MEADOW

PHOTOGRAPHED BY
KIM TAYLOR and **JANE BURTON**

WRITTEN BY
BARBARA TAYLOR

DK

DORLING KINDERSLEY, INC.

NEW YORK

A DORLING KINDERSLEY BOOK

Senior editor Christiane Gunzi **Senior art editor** Val Wright
Editor Deborah Murrell **Art editor** Julie Staniland
Design assistant Lucy Bennett
Production Louise Barratt
Illustrations Nick Hall
Index Jane Parker
Managing editor Sophie Mitchell
Managing art editor Miranda Kennedy
U.S. editor B. Alison Weir

Consultants
Andy Currant, Theresa Greenaway,
Paul Hillyard, Tim Parmenter, Edward Wade

With thanks to Trevor Smith's Animal World
for supplying some of the animals in this book.

Endpapers photographed by Hans Reinhard,
Bruce Coleman Ltd.

First American Edition, 1992
10 9 8 7 6 5 4 3 2 1
Published in the United States by
Dorling Kindersley, Inc., 232 Madison Avenue
New York, New York 10016

Library of Congress Cataloging-in-Publication Data
Taylor, Kim
Meadow/photographed by Kim Taylor and Jane Burton; written by
Barbara Taylor. – 1st American ed.
p. cm. – (Look closer)
Includes index
Summary: Examines some of the animals and plants found in meadows,
including the crab spider, partridge chicks, and cocksfoot grass.
ISBN 1-56458-129-2
1. Meadow fauna–Juvenile literature. 2. Meadow plants–Juvenile literature
[1. Meadow animals. 2. Meadow plants.]
I. Burton, Jane, ill. II. Taylor, Barbara, 1954- . III. Title. IV. Series.
QL115.5.T39 1992
574.909'53–dc20
92-52821–CIP–AC

Color reproduction by Colourscan, Singapore
Printed and bound in Italy by New Interlitho, Milan

CONTENTS

Look for us, and we will show you the size of every animal and plant that you read about in this book.

LIFE IN A MEADOW

DOTTED WITH COLORFUL FLOWERS and buzzing with insects, meadows are a rich habitat for wildlife. In summer, insects feed on the flowers, while larger animals such as mice and snakes climb and slither among the tall grasses. Many animals spend winter in the meadow in nests or burrows. Insect eggs stay buried in soil, and even seeds rest, sprouting only on warm, wet spring days. Most meadows were created many years ago, when people began to graze animals on the land and grow grasses to make hay. Today, many meadows have been plowed over so farmers can grow crops, with the help of chemicals. Wildlife finds it hard to survive in these fields. We need to protect our flower meadows so that wild plants and animals can keep their homes.

The stripe-winged grasshopper *(Stenobothrus lineatus)* is 1 in. long and lives in Europe.

The young slowworm *(Anguis fragilis)* is 3 in. long and lives in Asia and Europe.

The young harvest mouse's *(Micromys minutus)* body is 11/2 in. long and it lives in Europe.

Water avens *(Geum rivale)* flowers are 3/4 in. wide and grow in Europe, North America, and Western Asia.

Ragwort *(Senecio jacobaea)* flowers are 1 in. wide and grow in Europe, New Zealand, North Africa, North America, and Western Asia.

Field scabious *(Knautia arvensis)* flowers are 11/2 in. wide and grow in Europe and Western Asia.

The young grass snake *(Natrix natrix)* is 10 in. long and lives in Asia and Europe.

The cocksfoot grass's *(Dactylis glomerata)* seed head is 21/2 in. long and grows in Asia, North Africa, and Europe.

The common dung fly *(Scatophaga stercoraria)* is 1/2 in. long and lives in Asia, Europe, North Africa, and North America.

The bumblebee *(Bombus terrestris)* is 3/4 in. long and lives in Australia, Europe, North Africa, and North America.

Wood cranesbill *(Geranium sylvaticum)* flowers are 1 1/4 in. wide and grow in Europe, North America, and Siberia.

The damselfly *(Calopteryx virgo)* is 2 in. long and lives in Europe.

Dandelion *(Taraxacum officinale)* flowers are 1 1/4 in. wide and grow north of the Equator.

Red clover *(Trifolium pratense)* flowers are 1 1/4 in. wide and grow in Europe, New Zealand, North and South America, and Western Asia.

The cinnabar moth's *(Tyria jacobaeae)* wingspan is 1 1/4 in. and it lives in Europe and Western Asia.

Eggs of cinnabar moths are less than 1 mm wide.

The red-legged partridge chick *(Alectoris rufa)* is 3 in. high and lives in France, Spain, and the U.K.

The crab spider *(Misumena vatia)* is 1/2 in. long and lives in Europe, Japan, and North America.

The froghopper nymph *(Philaenus spumarius)* is 1/2 in. long and lives in Asia, Europe, and North America.

LEGLESS LIZARD

THIS SLITHERY SLOWWORM is not a worm, in spite of its name, but a kind of lizard. It looks like a worm because, unlike most lizards, it has no legs. Slowworms like to live in damp places, in long grass or leafy hedges, where they can hide from predators (enemies), such as snakes. Slowworms feed on slugs, snails, worms, and insects. In the cold winter months, when food is hard to find, they hibernate (sleep) in groups under tree roots, or in hollows in the ground. The female slowworm keeps her eggs inside her body until they are ready to hatch, then gives birth to between 12 and 20 live young.

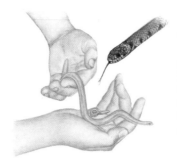

GUESS WHAT?
Both slowworms and grass snakes have long lives. Slowworms can live for more than 50 years, and grass snakes usually live for about 20 years.

WORN-OUT SKIN
The slowworm's scales are made of tough material. As this gradually wears away, a new set of scales grows beneath the outer one, and the old skin peels off the body. This is called sloughing. Most lizards slough their skin in several pieces, but slowworms shed their skin in one piece, like snakes.

The tiny scales fit closely together, so the body looks and feels smooth.

The long, thin body shape helps the slowworm to burrow easily into fallen leaves and soil.

SUN WORSHIPPER
Like all reptiles, slowworms have to soak up the warmth of the sun in order to gather enough energy to move and hunt. They are often found basking on warm, sunny banks. But on very hot days, they stay in the shade underneath flat stones, so the sun does not dry them out.

This pale collar gives grass snakes their other popular name. They are often called ringed snakes.

Snakes have no eyelids, so they cannot shut their eyes. They seem to be staring all the time.

Females and young slowworms, such as this one, have a dark belly and pale brown back.

The slowworm's rounded snout pushes aside soil, grass, and leaves as it slithers along.

The mouth is hinged so that it can open very wide. Grass snakes swallow their prey alive.

Eyelids keep the eyes clean.

The snake's forked tongue flicks in and out, tasting the air and picking up chemical information.

SWIMMING SNAKE
This snake is a good swimmer. It needs to be, because it feeds mainly on animals that live in or around water. Its streamlined body helps it slip easily and quickly through the water.

SNAKE IN THE GRASS

THE EUROPEAN GRASS SNAKE likes to bask in the sun, but disappears into the undergrowth when disturbed. It is sensitive to vibrations in the ground, which helps it avoid danger and catch food. Grass snakes mostly feed on frogs and newts, so they prefer to live in marshy meadows. These snakes hibernate in winter, under logs or in holes in the ground. In summer, the female lays her eggs in rotting plant material. This gives off heat, keeping the eggs and young snakes warm.

DEAD OR ALIVE

Grass snakes are not poisonous, but they can produce a very unpleasant smell to deter their enemies. They also wave their heads around and hiss loudly to make themselves look more frightening. Sometimes they even pretend to be dead, in the hope that their enemy will only attack living prey.

The snake's long, thin body helps it move fast, both in water and on land.

FLOWER POWER

MANY KINDS OF FLOWERING plants grow in meadows, including dandelions, buttercups, and clover. These wild flowers are often called weeds, because they grow quickly and do not need to be looked after. But they are just as attractive as the flowers that people grow in their gardens. Different kinds of meadows suit different plants. Water avens grows best in marshy meadows, and wood cranesbill grows well in alpine meadows. During the warm summer months, these plants produce flowers, which contain pollen and the sweet nectar that bees and butterflies like to eat. Meadow plants play an important part in providing food and shelter for many creatures, including insects, snails, and small mammals.

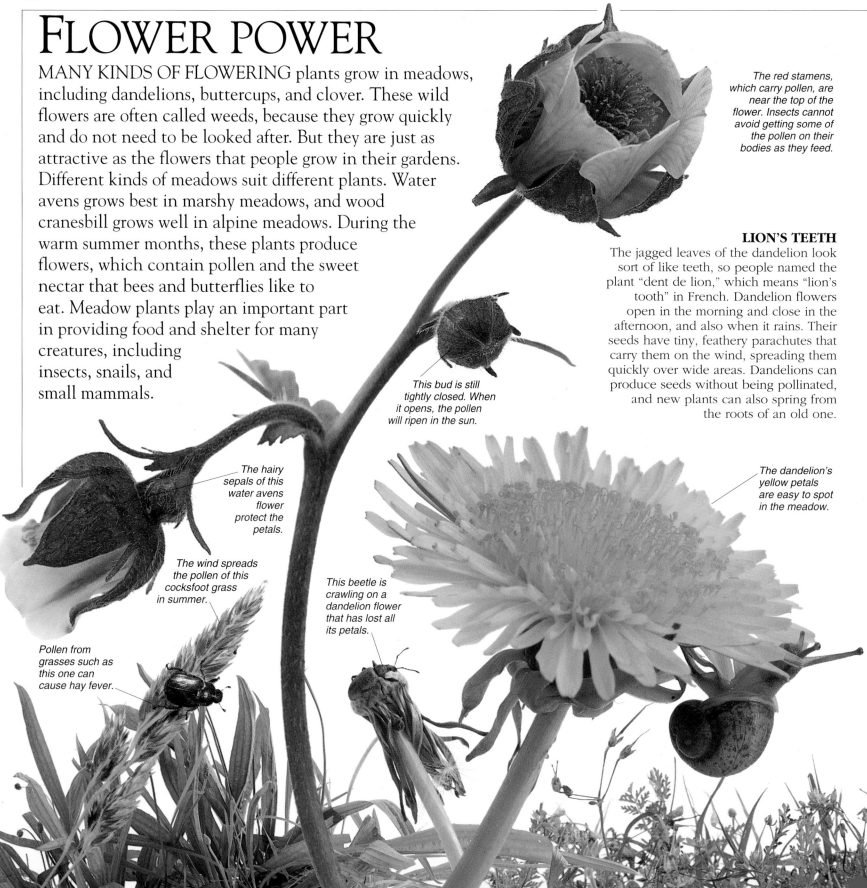

The red stamens, which carry pollen, are near the top of the flower. Insects cannot avoid getting some of the pollen on their bodies as they feed.

LION'S TEETH

The jagged leaves of the dandelion look sort of like teeth, so people named the plant "dent de lion," which means "lion's tooth" in French. Dandelion flowers open in the morning and close in the afternoon, and also when it rains. Their seeds have tiny, feathery parachutes that carry them on the wind, spreading them quickly over wide areas. Dandelions can produce seeds without being pollinated, and new plants can also spring from the roots of an old one.

This bud is still tightly closed. When it opens, the pollen will ripen in the sun.

The dandelion's yellow petals are easy to spot in the meadow.

The hairy sepals of this water avens flower protect the petals.

The wind spreads the pollen of this cocksfoot grass in summer.

This beetle is crawling on a dandelion flower that has lost all its petals.

Pollen from grasses such as this one can cause hay fever.

GUESS WHAT?
Several kinds of meadow flowers make tasty teas, and dandelion roots can be used to make coffee. But in spite of their delicate appearance, many flowers, including ragwort, are poisonous.

LATE DEVELOPERS
Ragwort, scabious, and several other meadow plants bloom in late summer or early autumn, when there are plenty of insects around to pollinate them. Several kinds of butterflies, including this European swallowtail, help spread the pollen. In return, the flowers provide nectar for the butterflies to eat.

POLLEN CARRIERS
As insects feed on meadow flowers, some of the pollen sticks to them. If it reaches another flower of the same kind, seeds which will produce new plants may develop. Many flowers produce pollen that is light enough to be carried on the wind, so they do not need insects to spread it.

The name "scabious" was given to this plant because people used to believe that it could cure a skin disease called scabies.

The nectar inside red clover flowers attracts bees. As they feed, the flower brushes pollen on to their fur.

The flower head of this ragwort is a cluster of many tiny flowers, called florets.

These two soldier beetles are shaped much like the petals of the ragwort flower that they are resting on.

A thick, strong stem supports the heavy flower head. Tiny hairs covering the stem discourage insects from eating it.

This wood cranesbill is so-named because when the fruits are mature, they look like the bill of a bird, called a crane.

MEADOW MONKEYS

TINY HARVEST MICE climb nimbly from one plant to another, like monkeys climbing through the trees of a forest. They spend most of the summer scampering around in the meadow, finding seeds and insects to eat. Harvest mice eat as much as they they can during the summer, then store the food energy as fat inside their bodies. In winter, they shelter from the cold in a nest. They only leave the nest during the warmer daylight hours, and spend more time on the ground, away from the wind. In spring, the female gives birth to between three and eight young. They have no fur at first, and cannot see or hear until they are nine days old. After about two weeks, they leave the nest. Many of the young only survive for a short time, because they are attacked by birds, toads, and weasels.

Big nostrils help the mouse to smell well, and avoid its enemies.

Short fur grows in a thick layer close to the body to keep the mouse warm.

CURLY TOES
Each foot has five toes. The large outer toe on each back foot can curl all the way around plant stems to give the mouse a firm grip. This special toe is much like a human thumb.

EMERGENCY CALL
Harvest mice make a shrill call, almost like a shriek, if they are in danger. Newborn harvest mice can also produce ultrasonic sounds, which are too high-pitched for us to hear. These calls quickly bring their parents to their rescue.

One toe on each of the front feet is so small that you can hardly see it at all.

These long, sharp claws help the harvest mouse grip plant stems.

This long toe works like a thumb to hold on to things.

Long, sensitive whiskers allow the mouse to feel its way in the dark.

Harvest mice have sharp hearing. They use their ears to listen for insects to eat, and for enemies to escape from.

A rounded snout hides teeth sharp enough to bite through leaves and stems.

EXTRA HAND

The harvest mouse can coil the end of its tail around anything, almost like an extra hand. This gives it added support when it is sitting or climbing in the grass. A harvest mouse can hang upside down on a stem by its tail alone. When the mouse climbs upward, it holds its tail stiffly out to help it keep its balance. Many kinds of monkeys also have a tail like this. It is called a prehensile tail.

Every hair on the mouse's body helps it feel things.

WEAVING A HOME

Harvest mice build nests for themselves and their young to shelter in. They bite blades of grass with their sharp teeth and weave them into a neat, round nest, about the size of a tennis ball. The mouse leaves the blades joined to the grass stems so that the nest hangs in midair. Inside is a cosy bed of finely chewed grass or thistle down to keep the mouse and its young warm.

The long tail is much less furry than the rest of the body. This allows it to grip things more easily.

GUESS WHAT?

Harvest mice are among the smallest mice in the world. A fully grown male weighs only a third of an ounce, and measures just 6 in. from its head to the end of its tail.

FLOWERS WITH FANGS

CRAB SPIDERS LURK among the colorful petals of meadow flowers, waiting for passing insects to land. A female crab spider's color often matches the flower that she lives on, so she can be very close to a victim without being spotted. When an insect lands on the flower to feed, the spider pounces on its prey. Crab spiders do not spin webs, but the females spin fluffy silk cocoons to protect their eggs. Inside each cocoon, there are 20 to 30 eggs which develop into tiny spiders, called spiderlings. They climb out of the cocoon after they have molted (shed their skin) for the first time. Each spiderling spins a silken thread and floats away on the wind to find a new home. Crab spiders live for about one year.

GUESS WHAT?
Some crab spiders have developed unusual kinds of camouflage. Tthey look like the ants they eat or the bird droppings that insects feed on.

SIDE STEPPER
Crab spiders are so-named because they tend to scuttle sideways, like crabs, instead of moving forward. Most crab spiders do not move very much. They spend their lives crouching on leaves, flowers, or tree trunks, waiting for their next meal to land.

The body is divided into two parts with a narrow waist, called a pedicel, in the middle.

This crab spider is well disguised against the ragwort flower that it lives on.

The front two pairs of legs, used for grabbing and holding prey, are longer and thicker than the other legs.

MATCHING CLOTHES
Many female crab spiders can change color to match different flowers. They may be white, brown, yellow, or even pink. It takes up to three days for the spider to change its color. When it stays very still on the flower, it is almost impossible for an insect to see it.

DEADLY AMBUSH

Crab spiders find their prey mainly by
sensing the vibrations (movements) of
an insect. When the insect is close
enough, the spider lunges out and
grabs it with its strong front legs.
Crab spiders often catch bees
and butterflies much larger
than themselves.

*This bee did not
see the crab
spider waiting to
pounce on it.*

*White crab
spiders often live
on the white
petals of
ox-eye daisies.*

*Close up, you can
see tiny hairs on
each leg, which
pick up vibrations
in the air.*

*The two leglike
palps are for
feeling.*

*These simple
black eyes are
tiny and cannot
see well.*

*This yellow crab
spider has climbed
on to a purple
cranesbill flower, so
flying insects will
probably see it and
avoid landing there.*

PARALYZING POISON

The spider bites its prey with two
fangs, which inject poison just behind
the victim's head. This paralyzes the
insect quickly and stops it from
struggling. Crab spiders have no teeth
to chew their prey, and may take
several hours to suck up the body
fluids. All that is left is an empty husk
with two holes made by the fangs.

*These jaws
have needlelike
fangs for injecting poison.*

*The huge abdomen
(rear part of the
body) makes
female crab spiders
easy to recognize.*

*Claws on each leg grip
prey and hold on to
slippery surfaces.*

GET UP AND GO

THESE FLUFFY partridge chicks can run around
just a few hours after hatching. They leave the
nest and join their parents in the hunt for
food. Both parents guard and protect the
chicks, and keep them safe and warm.
The chicks stay with the family group,
called a covey, until they are about a year
old. In spring, adult male partridges defend
their territory (the area in which they live)
against rival males. Then the male and female
partridges form pairs for mating. The female
partridge lays her eggs in a hollow in the ground in
tall grass or under a hedge. She sits on the eggs for
about three and a half weeks, to keep them warm until
they hatch. The color of her feathers blends in with the
shadowy background, so she is almost invisible to enemies.

*The ear openings
are on the sides
of the head.*

*Soft down traps
air next to the
skin, to keep the
bird warm.*

*The down has dark
and light stripes
that help hide the
young chick in the
undergrowth.*

*The wings are
still very small,
so the chick
can only flutter.*

*These long, clawed
toes are good for
gripping things and
scratching in the
soil for food.*

BALLS OF FLUFF
When partridge chicks hatch, they are
covered in soft, fluffy feathers, called
down. The down traps a layer of air next
to the chick's body to stop the warmth
from escaping its skin. The chicks start
growing adult feathers after about two
weeks, and have all their feathers at
about four weeks old. But they still have
down next to their skin to keep them
warm. The chicks can flutter at about 10
days old, and fly at 16 days old.

GUESS WHAT?
A female partridge lays
up to 25 eggs in one
clutch (batch), which is
more than any other
bird. Two or more birds
often lay their eggs
together, so there may
be more than 40 eggs
in one nest.

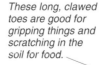

STRIPED FOR SAFETY
Striped markings break up the outline of the chick's body. This helps disguise chicks as they wander among the tall, thin meadow grasses. The stripes make it harder for enemies, such as weasels and foxes, to see them.

The speckled pattern on the eggs helps disguise them.

The eggshell is strong and waterproof, to prevent the chick inside from drying out.

When the chicks first hatch out, the down is wet from the liquid inside the egg. But it soon dries out, and fluffs up into a soft, warm coat.

Strong, flexible ankles allow the bird to bend easily to peck at the ground.

The short beak is useful for picking up food, such as flower seeds, from the ground.

This long toe on the foot points backward to help the chick keep its balance.

Close up, you can see the tough, scaly skin that protects the legs and feet.

BENDING BACKWARD
The chick's legs look as though they bend backward rather than forward at the knee. But the joint we can see bending is really the bird's ankle, not its knee, which is much closer to the body. Legs like this make it easier for the bird to bend down to pick up food from the ground.

FUZZY FLY

FURRY YELLOW dung flies spend much of their adult lives searching for cow or horse dung. They are very good at detecting the smell of the dung with their antennae. Male flies such as this one wait near the dung for females to arrive, then compete with each other to win a mate. The female lays her eggs inside the dung while it is still soft. When the legless larvae, called maggots, hatch out of the eggs, they feed on the dung. They develop in safety beneath the hard, protective crust which soon forms on it, then burrow into the soil and form pupae, from which winged adults emerge. These adults are flying around, ready to mate and lay eggs, as little as one month after they have hatched.

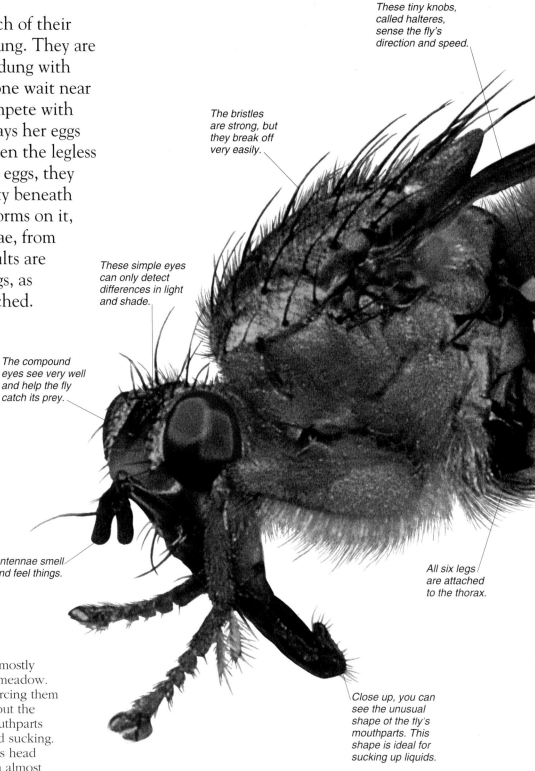

These tiny knobs, called halteres, sense the fly's direction and speed.

The bristles are strong, but they break off very easily.

These simple eyes can only detect differences in light and shade.

The compound eyes see very well and help the fly catch its prey.

Antennae smell and feel things.

All six legs are attached to the thorax.

Close up, you can see the unusual shape of the fly's mouthparts. This shape is ideal for sucking up liquids.

BRISTLING BACK

The dung fly has both hairs and bristles on its body. The stiff bristles on the back can feel solid objects, and help prevent the insect from damaging itself. The soft hairs covering the body are called cilia, and they can sense vibrations (movements) in the air, such as those of a nearby enemy. These hairs also trap a layer of air next to the fly's body, which helps keep it warm.

VAMPIRE FLY

Dung flies eat other insects, mostly flies, which they find in the meadow. They kill their victims by piercing them in the neck, then they suck out the body fluids. A dung fly's mouthparts are very good at piercing and sucking. The muscular pump inside its head allows it to suck liquids from almost any kind of food, living or dead.

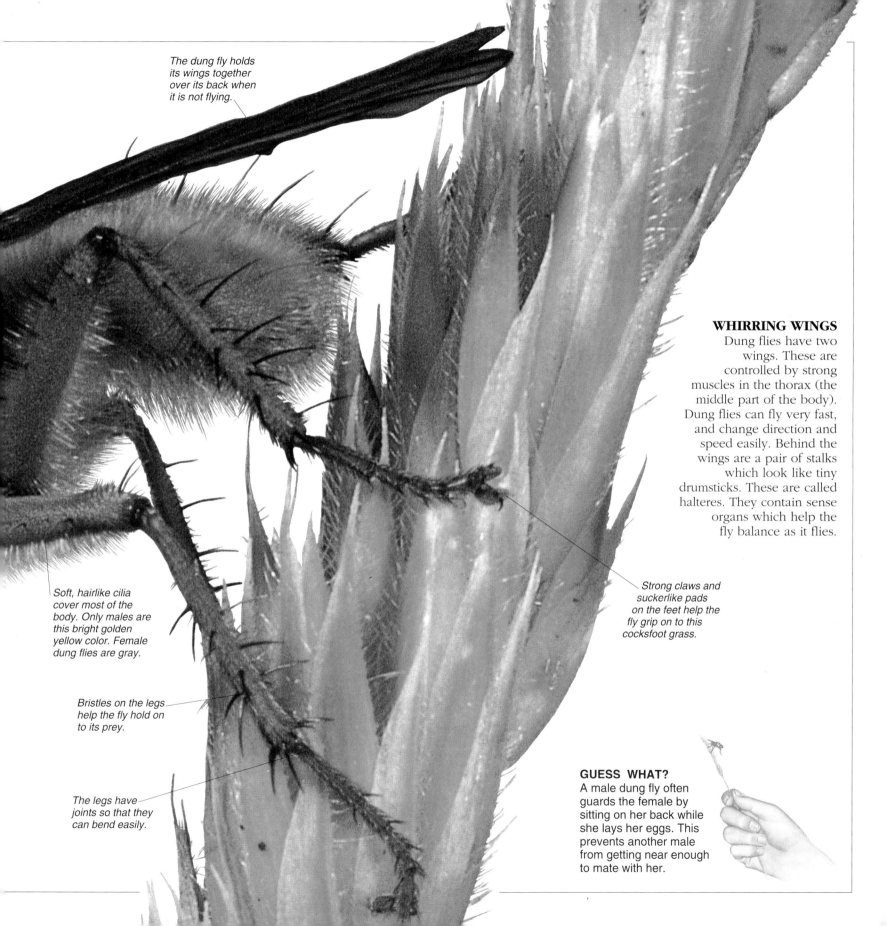

The dung fly holds its wings together over its back when it is not flying.

WHIRRING WINGS
Dung flies have two wings. These are controlled by strong muscles in the thorax (the middle part of the body). Dung flies can fly very fast, and change direction and speed easily. Behind the wings are a pair of stalks which look like tiny drumsticks. These are called halteres. They contain sense organs which help the fly balance as it flies.

Soft, hairlike cilia cover most of the body. Only males are this bright golden yellow color. Female dung flies are gray.

Strong claws and suckerlike pads on the feet help the fly grip on to this cocksfoot grass.

Bristles on the legs help the fly hold on to its prey.

The legs have joints so that they can bend easily.

GUESS WHAT?
A male dung fly often guards the female by sitting on her back while she lays her eggs. This prevents another male from getting near enough to mate with her.

DELICATE JEWEL

THIS SLENDER, DELICATE damselfly is related to the dragonfly, but it is a much less powerful flier. Damselflies fly slowly through waterside meadows on their flimsy wings, hunting for insects, such as gnats and midges, to eat. The female lays about 300 eggs in plant stems or leaves growing in or near water. She cuts a slit in the plant for the eggs with an egg-laying tube, called an ovipositor. Three weeks later, the eggs hatch into young, called nymphs, which live under water for about a year. They take in oxygen through gills at the tip of the abdomen (rear part of the body), and through their skin. The nymphs are fierce hunters of water insects, including other damselfly nymphs. When they are fully grown, they climb up a plant stem and out of the water. The skin splits and the adult damselfly pulls itself free and flies away.

The large, compound eyes are on each side of the head. Good eyesight is important for flying and catching food.

The head can turn easily on the slender neck, giving the insect a good all-around view.

Soft hairs on the body keep the damselfly warm.

The short antennae are sensitive to touch and smell.

Each foot has two hooks for holding on to slippery surfaces.

These hairs on the legs help the damselfly hold on to its prey.

TUBE FLOWER
The green sepals of this campion flower are joined to form a tube which protects the seeds. Above the sepals are five colorful petals which provide a useful resting place for a damselfly.

Once the flower is fertilized, this tube will hold the seeds until they are ripe.

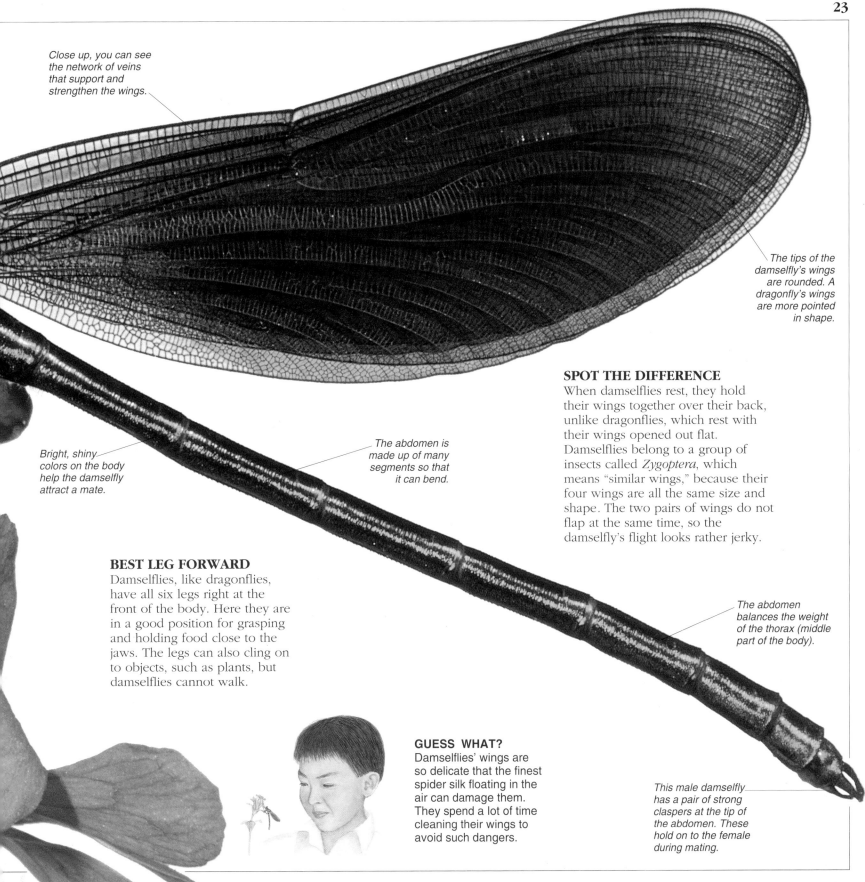

Close up, you can see the network of veins that support and strengthen the wings.

The tips of the damselfly's wings are rounded. A dragonfly's wings are more pointed in shape.

Bright, shiny colors on the body help the damselfly attract a mate.

The abdomen is made up of many segments so that it can bend.

SPOT THE DIFFERENCE

When damselflies rest, they hold their wings together over their back, unlike dragonflies, which rest with their wings opened out flat. Damselflies belong to a group of insects called *Zygoptera*, which means "similar wings," because their four wings are all the same size and shape. The two pairs of wings do not flap at the same time, so the damselfly's flight looks rather jerky.

BEST LEG FORWARD

Damselflies, like dragonflies, have all six legs right at the front of the body. Here they are in a good position for grasping and holding food close to the jaws. The legs can also cling on to objects, such as plants, but damselflies cannot walk.

The abdomen balances the weight of the thorax (middle part of the body).

GUESS WHAT?

Damselflies' wings are so delicate that the finest spider silk floating in the air can damage them. They spend a lot of time cleaning their wings to avoid such dangers.

This male damselfly has a pair of strong claspers at the tip of the abdomen. These hold on to the female during mating.

BLOWING BUBBLES

SMOOTH, GREEN froghopper nymphs such as this one live on plants, in blobs of white froth. They make the froth by blowing air into a sticky fluid that comes from their abdomen (the rear part of the body). The froth prevents the froghopper nymph from drying out, and protects it against enemies, such as birds, while it develops into an adult froghopper. Young nymphs have short antennae (feelers) and only the beginnings of wings, called wing buds. But during the spring, they molt (shed their skin) several times. By summer they have grown into adults, with full-size wings and antennae. Once they have wings to fly, they do not need the froth to protect them.

SAP SUCKERS
Froghopper adults and nymphs feed on the sap inside plant leaves and stems. They make tiny holes with their long, needlelike mouthparts, and suck up the sap.

Plant stems provide plenty of juicy sap for froghoppers and greenflies to feed on.

Aphids, such as these greenflies, often damage the plants they eat.

There is a froghopper nymph inside this blob of cuckoo spit.

FROTHY FROGS
Froghoppers are so named because the nymphs leap around like tiny frogs. The white blobs produced by young froghoppers are often called cuckoo spit, but they have nothing to do with cuckoos. The name comes from the fact that the frothy blobs appear at the same time as the cuckoo begins calling to attract a mate.

Large compound eyes detect danger.

Froghopper nymphs have short, bristle-like antennae.

These tiny wing buds will eventually develop into wings.

GREEDY GREENFLY
These tiny greenflies are related to froghoppers and, like them, they suck sap. Greenflies often live in large groups, and can cause a good deal of damage to the plants they live on, such as garden flowers or food crops.

GOLD DUST

BUMBLEBEES HELP carry the yellow dust called pollen from one meadow flower to another. In spring, a queen bee makes a nest out of grass and other plants, often in an old mouse hole. She lays her eggs in little wax cups, then sits on them to keep them warm. After a few days, most of them hatch into larvae (grubs). These feed on the nectar and pollen that the queen has stored in the nest. At about two weeks old, the grubs pupate (go into a resting stage), and then develop into adult worker bees like this one. Worker bees are females that do not mate or lay eggs, but only care for the queen and her young.

GUESS WHAT?
A bumblebee nest is about the size of a large grapefruit. In summer it is sometimes home to more than 200 bumblebees.

SWEET TOOTH
Bumblebees feed on the pollen and sugary nectar that flowers produce. The bees lick up their food with a long, pointed tongue. They only use their jaws to carry materials for building their nests.

HAIRY BASKET
Strong hairs on the bee's back legs form a sort of basket. The bee uses its front legs to comb the pollen from its body. Then it packs the pollen into the baskets to carry back to the nest. Bumblebees feed their young pollen because it contains protein, which helps them grow and develop.

The wings fold over the back when the bee is not flying.

Hairs trap a layer of warm air next to the bee's body.

This bee has collected lots of pollen in its pollen baskets.

Hooks on each foot grip leaves and petals.

WARM-UP EXERCISE
A furry coat helps keep the bee warm, but if it is cold, it shivers to warm up its wing muscles before taking off. Rows of tiny hooks link the front wings to the back wings for flying. This makes them function as one big wing, pushing the air aside more easily.

The bendable antennae sense things.

DON'T EAT ME

THE FRINGED BLACK and red wings of this cinnabar moth make it easy to recognize. When it flies around the meadow at night, these colors make it difficult to spot. But during the day, the wing coloring shows up well. It warns birds and other enemies that the insect tastes bad, so they leave it alone. Cinnabar moth caterpillars also taste unpleasant, and they have bright orange and black bands as their warning signal. They often feed together in such large numbers that they can strip plants, such as ragwort, completely bare. When the caterpillar is fully grown, it spins a silk cocoon in the soil or under fallen leaves, and turns into a pupa. It stays hidden away for the winter, and the adult moth does not emerge from the pupa until the following summer.

COLOR SCALES

The pattern on the wings is made from tiny, overlapping scales. Each scale is attached to the skin of the wing by a short stem. Moths belong to a group of insects called *Lepidoptera*, which means "scaled wing." Underneath the scales, the cinnabar moth's wings are transparent (clear), like those of bees, flies, and many other insects.

GUESS WHAT?
Sometimes a bird ignores the moth's warning colors and pccks at it. But the moth's body is so tough that little harm is done before the bird tastes the unpleasant fluid the insect produces.

These long, thin antennae can feel and smell things.

Like all insects, this moth has six jointed legs attached to the middle part of its body, called the thorax.

The large compound eyes are good at detecting movement. Each one has up to 6,000 separate lenses.

The bright colors warn enemies that this moth is not a tasty meal.

The front and back wings are joined together so they beat up and down at the same time.

Scales form a fringe around the edges of each wing.

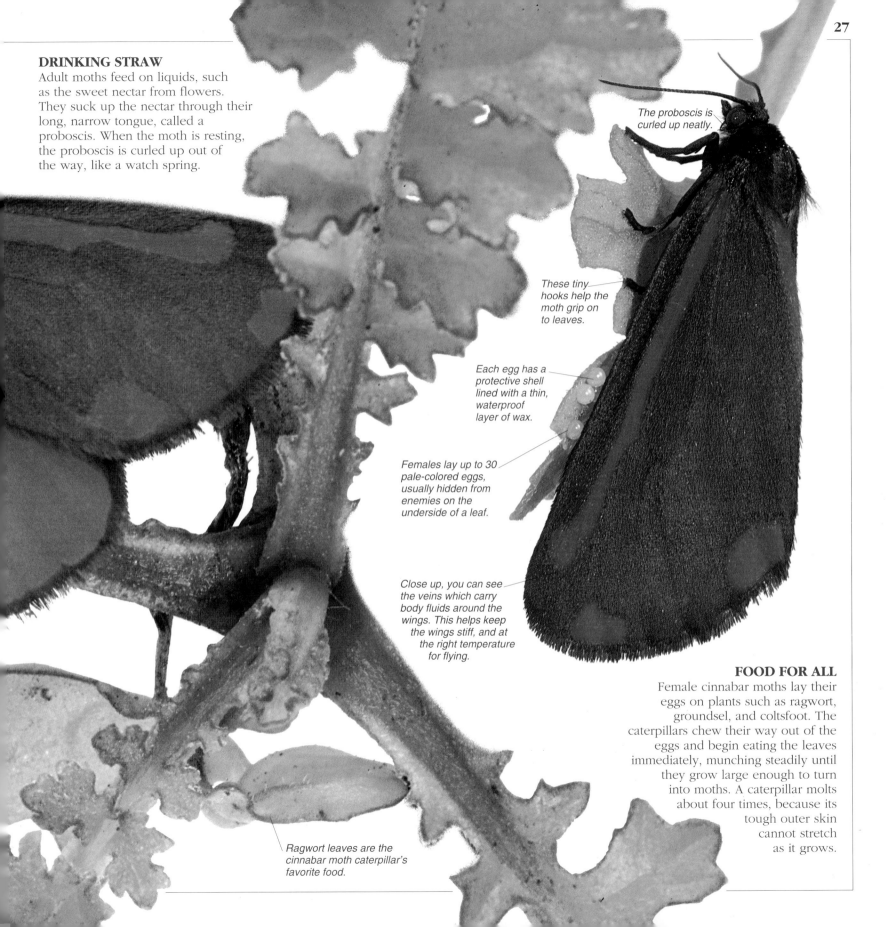

DRINKING STRAW

Adult moths feed on liquids, such as the sweet nectar from flowers. They suck up the nectar through their long, narrow tongue, called a proboscis. When the moth is resting, the proboscis is curled up out of the way, like a watch spring.

The proboscis is curled up neatly.

These tiny hooks help the moth grip on to leaves.

Each egg has a protective shell lined with a thin, waterproof layer of wax.

Females lay up to 30 pale-colored eggs, usually hidden from enemies on the underside of a leaf.

Close up, you can see the veins which carry body fluids around the wings. This helps keep the wings stiff, and at the right temperature for flying.

Ragwort leaves are the cinnabar moth caterpillar's favorite food.

FOOD FOR ALL

Female cinnabar moths lay their eggs on plants such as ragwort, groundsel, and coltsfoot. The caterpillars chew their way out of the eggs and begin eating the leaves immediately, munching steadily until they grow large enough to turn into moths. A caterpillar molts about four times, because its tough outer skin cannot stretch as it grows.

LEGGY LEAPER

A STRIPE-WINGED grasshopper is difficult to spot when it is sitting still among the meadow grasses. If necessary, it can speedily leap away from enemies, such as birds and spiders, on its long back legs. Grasshoppers eat mostly plants, cutting and grinding up grasses with their sharp, jagged mandibles (jaws). In summer, the female lays her eggs around the roots of grasses, or just under the soil. She covers them with a frothy liquid that hardens to protect the eggs through the cold months. Tiny wormlike larvae hatch out in spring. They instantly molt (shed their skin) to become nymphs, which look much more like adults. The nymphs molt three more times as they grow into full-sized adults.

GUESS WHAT?
This grasshopper can jump about 12 in. off the ground, which is almost 40 times its own height. When alarmed, it can combine jumping and flying to travel up to 9 ft. away.

A CLEVER ESCAPE
If the grasshopper is caught by one of its rear legs, it can break off the leg in order to escape from its enemy. There is a special muscle at the base of the leg which snaps it off the body, and the wound seals immediately.

This hard, saddle-shaped collar is called a pronotum. It protects the front part of the body.

Young grasshoppers such as this one cannot fly because their wings are not yet fully developed.

The abdomen is made up of many segments with joints between them, so it can bend easily.

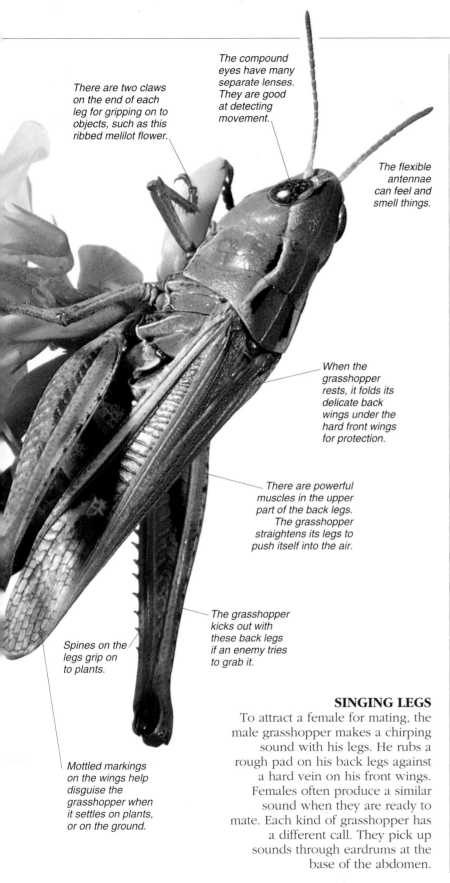

There are two claws on the end of each leg for gripping on to objects, such as this ribbed melilot flower.

The compound eyes have many separate lenses. They are good at detecting movement.

The flexible antennae can feel and smell things.

When the grasshopper rests, it folds its delicate back wings under the hard front wings for protection.

There are powerful muscles in the upper part of the back legs. The grasshopper straightens its legs to push itself into the air.

The grasshopper kicks out with these back legs if an enemy tries to grab it.

Spines on the legs grip on to plants.

Mottled markings on the wings help disguise the grasshopper when it settles on plants, or on the ground.

SINGING LEGS

To attract a female for mating, the male grasshopper makes a chirping sound with his legs. He rubs a rough pad on his back legs against a hard vein on his front wings. Females often produce a similar sound when they are ready to mate. Each kind of grasshopper has a different call. They pick up sounds through eardrums at the base of the abdomen.

GLOSSARY

Abdomen *the rear part of the body*
Antennae *a pair of feelers*
Camouflage *the colors and patterns of an animal that match its background*
Cilia *short, hairlike threads*
Cocoon *a bag that an insect pupa makes from silk in which to develop*
Compound eyes *eyes consisting of many separate lenses*
Hibernate *to rest or sleep during the cold months of the year*
Larva *the young, grublike stage of an animal's life*
Molt *to shed the skin or exoskeleton*
Nectar *the sweet liquid that flowers produce, and which many insects drink*

Nymph *the larva of certain kinds of insects, such as damselflies*
Prehensile tail *a tail that can grasp*
Proboscis *the long, strawlike mouthpart of a butterfly or moth*
Pupa *the resting stage between a larva and an adult insect*
Sepal *one of the outer parts of a flower that protects the bud*
Sloughing *molting (snakes and lizards)*
Thorax *the middle part of the body, containing the heart and lungs*
Ultrasonic *a sound that is too high for humans to hear*
Vibrations *tiny movements in air, in water, or underground*